يُؤْتِى ٱلْحِكْمَةَ مَن يَشَآءُ وَمَن يُؤْتَ ٱلْحِكْمَةَ فَقَدْ أُوتِىَ خَيْرًا كَثِيرًا وَمَا يَذَّكَّرُ إِلَّآ أُوْلُوا۟ ٱلْأَلْبَٰبِ ﴿٢٦٩﴾

He gives wisdom to whoever he wants – and whoever is given wisdom has been given tremendous good.

MY DEAR CHILD

By

The Imam, the faith-reviver, the proof of Islam and the Muslims

Zainudden Abu Haamid

Muhammad ibn Muhammad ibn Muhammad ibn Ahmad

Al-Ghazali

Of Tus and Tabaran

And of the Shafi Madhab

May Allah be pleased with him

(450 – 505 AH)

In the name of Allah, most gracious, most merciful

He is the one we call on for help

All praise is due to Allah, lord of the worlds, and the ultimate good is for the godfearing ones, and peace and blessings be upon His messenger Muhammad (saw), his family and all his companions.

CONTEXT

An old student who had stayed in the service of Sheikh Imam Zainudeen (the Proof of Islam) Abu Haamid Muhammad ibn Muhammad Al-Ghazali (May Allah have mercy on him), had busied himself acquiring knowledge from him, until he had mastered the most difficult of subjects, and conquered his self.

Then one day, he paused and reflected, and was fearful for himself. He thought, "I have studied so many subjects, and have spent by life learning them and mastering them, but now I need to know which ones will benefit me in the next life, and give me comfort once I have died. And which ones are of no benefit to me, so that I can avoid them. The prophet (saw) has said: "O Allah! I seek your protection from useless knowledge.""

 This concern continued to trouble him, until he wrote to the honoured sheikh, the proof of Islam, Muhammad al Ghazali, May Allah have mercy on him, for answers. He asked him a number of questions, and requested some advice and prayers.

He says, "Even though the books authored by Imam Ghazail like Ihya uloom ud deen contain the answers to my questions, my aim was to have the Sheikh write a few pages in answer to my questions, so that those pages may remain with me for as long as I live, and that I may act upon what is in them for as long as I live, *inshallah.*"

IMAM GHAZALI
REPLIES

Imam Ghazali wrote the following letter in reply.

MY DEAR RESPECTED CHILD!

May Allah keep you steadfast in your obedience to Him, and may He help you to tread the path of those He loves.

The flowers of good advice are taken from the treasures of the Hadith of the Prophet (saw). When you have received the advice directly from there, why is there a need to take it from me?

If you haven't yet come across the advice, then ask yourself: what have you been doing all these years?

MY DEAR CHILD

From the multitude of advice that the Prophet (saw) has given his Ummah, are the words:

"A sign of Allah turning away from a slave, is that he is busy in useless activities."

"If a person spends even a moment of his life in activities unrelated to the reasons for which he was created, then he has a right to show continued remorse."

"Anyone who reaches the age of 40 in such a state that his good deeds are less than his evil deeds should prepare to go to Hell."

These pieces of advice are sufficient (to change behaviour) for someone with intellect.

MY DEAR CHILD

Giving advice is easy – what's difficult is accepting it and acting on it. This is because good advice feels bitter to those who follow their desires, because they find forbidden acts attractive.

This is especially the case for traditional students who are busy seeking praise and fame, who think that knowledge alone is sufficient as a means for success, and there is no need for action, when in fact, such belief is the belief of the (wayward) philosophers.

Subhanallah, astonishing! This person doesn't even realise that when he gains some knowledge, then fails to act upon it, that knowledge will be a witness against him in the hereafter. The Prophet (saw) has said: **"The person who will be most severely punished on the Day of Judgement will be a scholar who failed to benefit from his knowledge."**

It has been narrated that after his death, Junaid (of Baghdad) (rh) was seen in a dream. He was asked, "Give us some news, O Abul Qasim." He replied, **"Deep study and insightful knowledge failed me. But a few units of prayer, offered in the middle of the night, were the only thing to benefit me."**

MY DEAR CHILD

Do not lack in deeds, or be empty of character, and know for certain that knowledge on its own will not take you (into paradise) by the hand.

For example, imagine a person crossing through some wild land. He carries 10 (sharp) Indian swords, in addition to lots of other weaponry. This man is brave, and skilled at the art of war. If a lion were to suddenly pounce on him, what do you think would happen?

Will the weapons ward off the evil (of the lion) if they are left unused, and he doesn't strike with them? We all know for certain that the lion can only be fended off with action and striking.

Similarly, if a person reads up on 100,000 religious problems and their solutions, and learns them and teaches them, but doesn't act on them, then they won't benefit him until he acts upon them.

Another example is a person suffering for heat and yellow fever. His cure lies in using a mixture of vinegar and honey, or barley water. He will only get better if he drinks it. A Persian saying is:

كَرْ مَيْ دُو هَزَار رِطْل پَيْمايي   تا مَيْ نَخُوري نَبا شَدَتْ شيدايي

If you weigh 2 thousand litres of wine, you
won't be drunk until you drink it.

If you were to read books for a hundred years, and had a collection of a thousand books, you would only be worthy of Allah's mercy through action. Allah says, "A person will have only what he strives for."

If anyone claims that this verse has been abrogated, because of the Prophet (saw)'s saying "when a person dies, all his deeds end except 3 ..." then the thing that is abrogated is the speaker (ie ignore him).

If it were abrogated, then how do you explain the verses: "Whoever has hope in meeting his lord, should perform good deeds," or "a reward for the deeds that you did" or "a reward for what you earned," or "indeed those who believed and performed good deeds will have Paradise as a home" and "...except those who repented, believed and performed good deeds."

And what do you say about the hadith "Islam is founded upon 5 (key ideas): 1) bearing witness that there is no God except Allah and that Muhammad is his messenger, 2) performing salah, 3) giving Zakah, 4) fasting in Ramadhan and 5) performing Hajj for those who are able to."

Imaan, or faith, is a combination or saying so with words, belief in the heart and acting up on the key acts of Islam.

The proofs for the importance of action are far too many to be counted. If a servant of Allah reaches Paradise through the bounty and grace of Allah, this will be after he has prepared for it by obeying and worshipping him, because "the mercy of Allah is close to those who perform good deeds."

If it is claimed: "A person can reach Paradise through belief alone," we reply, "Yes, but when will he reach there? How many uphill struggles will he face until he reaches there. The first struggle is the struggle of Iman, or faith – will he even cross over (into the next life) with his faith intact, or will he have lost it? And even if he reaches Paradise, he will be a bankrupt resident of Paradise.

Hasan al-Basri (rh) says: "Allah will tell his servants on Judgement Day, 'Enter Paradise as a consequence of my mercy, and distribute it amongst yourselves based upon the good deeds you amassed'".

MY DEAR CHILD

Without action, you will have no reward.

There is a story about a person from the Banu Israeel who continuously worshipped Allah for 70 years. Allah wanted to reveal his status to the angels, so Allah sent an angel to inform the man that "Despite your worship, you have no right to Paradise."

Once the angel had told the man, he replied, "We have been created to worship Allah, so it is appropriate for us to do only that."

Once the angel returned to Allah, Allah asked him, "What did my servant say?". The angel replied, "My Lord! You know best what your servant has said!" Allah then said, "He will not turn away from worshipping me, and I, through my mercy, will not turn away from him. Bear witness, O angels, that I have forgiven him."

The Prophet (saw) has said, "Hold yourself accountable (in this life), before you are held accountable (in the next life), weigh your (good and bad) deeds (in this life), before they are weighed for you."

Ali (ra) said, "Whoever believes that he can reach Paradise without effort, is a dreamer, and whoever believes he will reach paradise through effort alone, is arrogant."

Hasan (rh) said: "Wanting Paradise, but failing to do anything about it, is a sin."

He also said, "True obedience to Allah is that a slave stops considering his deeds as great, but still continues to do them."

The Prophet (saw) has said, "The smart person is the one who suppresses his desire, and works for what is to come after death, and the foolish person is the one who follows the desires of his soul, then continues to have hope in Allah."

MY DEAR CHILD

So many nights you have spent awake, revising what you had been taught, and reading books around your subjects. You stopped yourself from sleeping, but what was the reason for that?

If your intention was to attain a piece of this world, and to gather its rubbish, to gain a high status and to show your superiority over your peers, then you are condemned, you are condemned!

But if your aim was to spread the shariah and way of the Prophet (saw), to improve your own character and manners, and to suppress this soul of yours that calls you to evil, then rejoice, rejoice, rejoice!

A poet spoke the truth when he said:

When these eyes are awake for anyone other than you, then they
are being wasted
And when they cry at being distanced from anyone
other than you, they are being completely wrong

MY DEAR CHILD

Live as you wish, but remember: you will eventually die

Love who you want, but remember: the two of you will one day separate

Do whatever you want, but remember: you will be recompensed for your actions.

MY DEAR CHILD

What is the point of studying logic, debates, medicine, poetry, astronomy, grammar and morphology (if it isn't used for religious benefit, and if you don't act upon it) – it is just a waste of time. You are simply attaining the displeasure of the Almighty.

I read in the Injeel of Isa (as) that he said: "From the moment that a body is put on the coffin, until it is placed in the grave, Allah Almighty asks him 40 questions. The first is that Allah says, "O my slave! You spent many years making yourself look beautiful for the people, but you didn't spend a single moment making yourself look good for me (improving your character and manners) – and every day, I look at your heart!"

Allah says, "What is the point of turning to others, when you are surrounded by my blessings. Are you deaf? Can you not hear?"

MY DEAR CHILD

Knowledge without action is madness, and action without knowledge cannot happen. Bear in mind that knowledge will not keep you away from sin, nor will it cause you to become obedient, and nor will it distance you from the Fire of Jahannam.

If you fail to act now, and do not make up for the days you have lost, then tomorrow, on the Day of Standing, you will say, "Send us back! We will perform good deeds," and you will be told, "O Fool! It is from that very place that you came!"

MY DEAR CHILD

Make your soul strong, fight against your desires, and remember that death is near. Your final destination is the grave, and the grave-dwellers await you all the time, asking when you will be joining them.

So beware! Beware of joining them empty-handed of provisions (good deeds).

Abu Bakr siddiq (ra) said: **"These bodies are either cages for birds, or pens for cattle."**

SO reflect and ask yourself, which one are you?

If you are of the lofty birds, then when (at the time of death) you hear the radiating sound of "Return to your Lord!" you will fly out, rising until you settle at the highest towers of Paradise. Like the Prophet (saw) said: **"The throne of Allah shook (in excitement and happiness) at the death of Saa'd ibn Muadh."**

And – May Allah protect us – if you are of the cattle, then like Allah has said: **"They are like animals; no, they are more astray than animals,"** you are not safe from going direct from the corners of this world, to the pits of Hell.

It has been narrated that Hasan Basri (rh) was given some cold water to drink. When he took the glass of water, he passed out, and the glass fell from his hand.

Once he came round, he was asked, "What happened, O Abu Saeed?" He replied, **"The cravings of the citizens of hell came to mind, when they will ask the citizens of Paradise, "Pour us some water, or give us some of what your Lord has provided you."**

MY DEAR CHILD

If knowledge alone were sufficient for you, and you had no need for any other deed, The words of Allah "Does anyone have a request? Does anyone want to be forgiven? Does anyone want to repent?" would have been wasted and of no benefit.

It has been narrated that the group of Sahaba (ra) spoke highly of Abdullah ibn Umar (ra) in front of the Prophet (saw). The Prophet (saw) then said: "What a wonderful person he is. If only he would pray at night."

And the Prophet (saw) told one of his companions, "Don't sleep too much at night, because too much sleep at night will leave a person poor on Judgement Day."

MY DEAR CHILD

Allah says, "Perform the Tahajjud prayer at night," – this is a command.

Allah says, "Before dawn, they seek forgiveness." - this is gratitude.

Allah says, "They are seeking forgiveness before dawn." – this is a reminder.

The Prophet (saw) has said, "There are 3 sounds that Allah loves: the sound of a rooster (that wakes people up for Fajr), the sound of the one who reads Quran, and the sound of those who seek forgiveness before dawn."

Sufyan Thawri (ra) said, "Allah has created a wind that blows before dawn, and carries the dhikr (praise of Allah) and istighfaar (requests for forgiveness) to the Mighty King, Allah."

He also said, "When the night begins, a caller calls out from under the throne of Allah, 'Listen! Let the worshippers arise,' so they stand, and pray whoever much Allah wants them to pray."

"Then a caller calls out in the middle of the night, 'Listen! Let the obedient ones arise,' so they stand, and pray until close to dawn.

"Then when dawn arrives, a caller calls out 'Listen! Let those who seek forgiveness arise,' so they stand, and ask Allah for forgiveness."

"Then, once dawn has broken, a caller calls out, 'Listen! Let the heedless ones arise,' so they rise from their beds like dead people who have been resurrected from their graves."

MY DEAR CHILD

It has been seen that one of the pieces of advice that Luqman the Wise gave to his son was, "My dear son, do not let the rooster be smarter than you. He calls out before dawn, while you are still asleep."

How wonderful are the words of the one who said:

In the midst of the night, the pigeon twitters	Sitting upon a branch, while I am in a deep sleep
I swear by the house of Allah, I am lying. Were I truly devoted to Allah,	The pigeon would not have beaten me to crying first
Am I really a truly devoted servant to my lord,	when I do not cry, whilst even the animals cry

MY DEAR CHILD

The essence of learning is that you understand what obedience and worship truly are.

Remember that obedience and worship are following the commands of, and refraining from the prohibitions set by, the lawgiver Allah, in speech and action – in everything you say or don't say, and everything you do or don't do. For example, if you fasted on the 2 days of Eid, or the days of tashreeq (following Eid ul-Adha), you would be sinful. Similarly, if you performed your prayers using stolen clothes, even though ostensibly, you were engaged in worship, you would actually be sinning.

MY DEAR CHILD

Your speech and actions should be in in line with the Shariah. Knowledge and action that contradict the shariah are waywardness.

Do not be led astray by the unevidenced interpretations and wild statements of the (false) Sufis, because treading this path requires tremendous effort, including the suppression of one's desires, and killing its wishes with the sword of contentment, and not by wild cliams and fairy tales.

Remember that a loose tongue and heart that is surrounded by and filled with indifference and cravings indicates an unfortunate person. Only after you kill off the cravings of your soul with true effort will your heart become alive with the lights of true appreciation of Allah.

Remember that some of the questions you asked me cannot be answered by writing to you about them or discussing them with you. Instead, if you ever reach that stage, you will understand the answers, and if not, then true knowledge of them is impossible. This is because they must be experienced – and anything that needs to be experienced cannot be fully described with words, just like the sweetness of something sweet, and the bitterness of something bitter, can only be understood by tasting them.

It's like the story of the impotent man who wrote to his friend and asked him, "Describe the pleasure of copulation to me. What is it like."

His friend wrote back, "I originally thought you were just impotent, but now I realise you are both impotent and stupid. This pleasure is experienced. Only if you experience it, will you understand it, and if not, it cannot be explained in speech or in writing."

MY DEAR CHILD

Some of the questions you asked are like this.

But there were some that could be answered – I have answered them in Ihya al uloom and other books, but I will mention some extracts here, and provide reference to others.

The first question you asked me was about the seeker of Allah is obligated to do.

I say: there are 4 things the seeker of Allah must do:

1) Have correct aqeedah, or set of beliefs. There should be no aberrant views held.
2) Genuine repentance – and he shouldn't slip up afterwards either.
3) Make those who he has made unhappy, happy, so that no one is left with rights over him.
4) Gain enough knowledge of the shariah, the laws of Allah, so that he can correctly fulfil the commands of Allah - He is not obligated to learn more than this – and he must also learn those things connected with the hereafter that will result in him being saved (from the fire of Hell).

It has been narrated that Shibli (rh) worked under 400 teachers. He said, "I have studied 4000 hadiths, and from them, I chose one hadith that I act upon, and put the rest to the side, because I reflected on them, and I concluded that I could be saved from the Hellfire, and be successful through this single hadith. The knowledge of the earlier and later communities is subsumed by it, so I sufficed with it.

And that hadith is that the Prophet (saw) told some of his companions, **"Work that hard for your worldly life, according to** how long you will stay in it, and work that hard for your life hereafter, according to how long you will stay there. Worship Allah according to how much you need him, and work to save yourself from the fire of Hell according to how much patience you would be able to bear if you ended up in it."

MY DEAR CHILD

Once you act upon this hadith, you will realise you don't need a mass of knowledge.

And think deeply about another story:

Hatim al-Asamm was close to and a student of Shaqeeq al-Balkhi (rh). One day Shaqeeq (rh) asked him: "You've been with me for 30 years – what have you learnt from me?"

He replied: "I have learnt 8 pieces of knowledge from you and they are enough for me, because I believe I will be saved and successful because of them."

Shaqeeq (rh) asked, "What are they?"

Hatim (rh) replied:"

1) I looked at the people, and I realised that every one of them had people who loved them deeply. Some of those people he was close to stayed with him until he died, and others accompanied him to the edge of his grave.

   Then every single one left him, and he was all alone. No one stayed in the grave with him.
   So I thought about this and concluded that the best friend a person can have is the one that joins him in the grave and comforts him there, and I found that to be good deeds alone, and so I made them by best friend, so that they may be a light for me in the grave, and may comfort me when I am there, and will never abandon me.

2) I saw the people following their whims and rushing to satisfy the cravings of their soul.

I thought about the words of Allah, "And as for that person who fears standing before his Lord, and stops the cravings of his soul, then Paradise will be his resting place." I then realised how true and correct the Quran is.

Thus, I immediately began to do the opposite of what my soul desired, and prepared to work hard against it, and never submitted to whatever my soul wanted, until it became happy to obey Allah, and submitted to worship.

3)   I saw everyone rushing to gather up the rotten wood of this world (wealth), and then holding onto it tightly.

I thought about the words of Allah, "What you have will come to an end but what Allah has will remain."

So whatever possessions I had, I gave away, seeking the pleasure of Allah, distributing them amongst the poor, so that they may become treasure for me when I am with Allah the Almighty.

4)   I saw some people believing that honour and respect lay in knowing lots of people, and they boasted about it.

Others believed it lay in having lots of wealth or children, so they bragged about it.

Others believed that honour and respect lay in stealing people's wealth, oppressing them and spilling their blood.

And some people believed it lay in destroying property, wasting money and an extravagant lifestyle.

I thought about the words of Allah, "The most honourable amongst you is the one who is the most pious."

Therefore, I chose piety, and fully realised that the Quran is completely true, and the thoughts and opinions of the people are all completely false and temporary.

5)   I saw people criticising each other, and gossiping about each

other. I realised this was because of their wealth, their fame or their knowledge.

I thought about the words of Allah, "We have distributed their sustenance between them in the life of this world."

I realised that this distribution is from Allah and is pre-determined, so I was never jealous of anyone, and happy with the Allah's distribution.

6)   I saw people in conflict with one another for some reason or other.

I thought about the words of Allah, "Satan is your enemy, so treat him like an enemy."

I realised that it is not permissible to hate anyone other than Satan, so I made him my enemy, and left everyone else.

7)   I saw people trying so hard, and really straining themselves, to earn some resources or income such that they would fall into doubtful and haram activities, disgrace themselves and debase themselves.

I thought about the words of Allah, "Allah is responsible for the provisions of every animal on the earth."

I realised that Allah is responsible for my income, and he has promised to provide it, so I focused on worshipping Him, and stopped depending on others.

8)   I saw that everyone was dependent on someone or something.

- Some people were dependent on dinars and dirhams (money)
- Others on commodities and properties
- Others on handiwork and manufacturing
- Others were dependent on fellow human beings.

So I thought about the words of Allah, "Whosoever places his trust in Allah, then Allah is sufficient for him. Allah will get the matter completed. Allah has made everything in proportion."

So I placed my trust in Allah; He is sufficient for me, and an excellent supporter.

Shaqeeq (rh) then said, "May Allah make you successful, O Hatim! I have read the Torah, Injeel, Zabur and Quran, and I found all 4 books covering these 8 points – so whoever acts upon them is acting upon the teachings of all 4 books.

MY DEAR CHILD

You will have learnt from these 2 stories that you don't need a mass of knowledge (but in fact need lots of action and deeds). I'm now going to explain to you what a person seeking the path to the truth must have with him.

The seeker must have a sheikh to guide and develop him, to remove the poor characteristics from him with *tarbiyah*, through support, and replace them with good characteristics.

What is the meaning of *tarbiyah*? It is like the actions of a farmer who pulls out the weeds and other invasive species of plants from the field, so that his crops grow well, and the harvest is maximised.

The seeker needs a sheikh to help him grow, and guide him to the path of Allah, because Allah sent messengers to his servants to guide them, but when the Prophet (saw) left this world, the caliphs that came after him took on this role in his place, so that they may guide the masses towards Allah.

For a sheikh to be competent enough to stand in for the Prophet (saw), he must be of considerable religious knowledge (an alim), but not every alim is fit to be a guiding sheikh.

I will now summarise for you some of the characteristics of a guiding sheikh, so that not everyone can lay claim to being a guiding sheikh.

1) He is someone who turns away from the world and from fame.
2) He is a disciple of another guiding sheikh,
3) He has a chain going back to the Prophet (saw).
4) He is constantly doing good work

5) He works hard on his self.
6) He doesn't eat or drink much
7) He doesn't talk much
8) He doesn't sleep much
9) He prays lots of optional prayers
10) He gives a lot of optional charity
11) He keeps a lot of optional fasts

In following his guiding sheikh, he imbibes within himself the good characteristics of:

12) Patience
13) Gratitude
14) Trust in Allah
15) Firm faith
16) Generosity
17) Contentment
18) Composure
19) Tolerance
20) Humility
21) knowledge
22) honesty
23) modesty
24) trustworthiness
25) respect
26) calmness
27) careful thought etc.

Such an individual is a light from the lights of the Prophet (saw) and is suitable for following. However, it is rare to find such an individual –rarer than red sulphur.

Whoever is fortunate enough to find such a sheikh, and the sheikh then accepts him, should respect him both in public and in private.

Public respect is that:

- He does not argue with him, and does not try to prove him wrong in any situation, even if he believes (through his

incomplete knowledge) that the sheikh is wrong.
- He does not place a prayer mat in front of him unless it is time for prayer, and once he has prayed, he folds it up again.
- He doesn't pray excessive amounts of optional nafl prayers in front of him.
- He does what the sheikh tells him to do, according to his ability.

Private respect is that:
- Everything he hears from his sheikh, and which he accepted in public, he does not reject in private, neither in action nor in speech, so that he is not branded a hypocrite. If he is unable to do this, he should separate from his sheikh until he is the same in private and in public.
- He stays away from gatherings of the sinful ones, to reduce the impact of wretched jinns and wretched people on the depths of his heart, and so that he is kept pure from the filth of Satan.
- In all situations, he chooses poverty over wealth

In addition, know that Sufism has 2 key components: *istiqaamah*, or consistency, and *sukoon anil khalq*, being gentle to the people. Thus, whoever is consistent and is well mannered with the people and treats them mildly, then HE is a sufi.

Istiqaamah is that he sacrifices the desires he has (for the sake of the hereafter).

Being well mannered with the people is that he doesn't force them to do what he desires, but rather, he tries to accommodate them, as long as their wishes do not contravene the shariah, the laws of Allah.

You also asked me about *ubudiyyah* (being a true servant of Allah). It has 3 parts to it:

1) To consistently follow the commands of the shariah
2) To be happy with the Allah's decree, destiny and distributions

3) To sacrifice your happiness and pleasure to gain the approval of Allah.

You asked me about *tawakkul*. *Tawakkul* is that you have a firm belief in Allah that he will do what he has promised. In other words, you believe firmly that you will undoubtedly receive whatever has been decreed for you, even if the rest of the world attempts to divert it from you, and that whatever has not been decreed for you will not reach you, even if the rest of the world were to help you achieve it.

You asked me about *Ikhlaas*. *Ikhlaas* is that every deed you do is to seek the approval of Allah. Your heart does not seek the praises of the people, nor are you bothered by the criticisms.

Know that *riyaa*, or trying to impress others and showing off to them, is caused by believing in the greatness of people. The solution is view them as being under the control of Allah. Think of them as being like inanimate objects, unable to grant help or cause difficulty, so that you may purify yourself from showing off. For as long as you view the people as having power and choice, you are always at risk of showing off to them and attempting to impress them.

MY DEAR CHILD

As for the rest of your questions, some of the answers are written in my books, so look for the answers there, whilst others I mustn't write about.

Act upon what you have learnt, so that what you don't know makes sense to you. The Prophet (saw) has said, "Whoever acts upon the knowledge he has, Allah will give him the knowledge of what he doesn't know."

MY DEAR CHILD

After today, ask me about the problems you face only through the tongue of your heart (in other words, don't write to me, just think about the answers). Allah says, "If they had waited until you came out to them, it would have been better for them."

Accept the advice of Sayyiduna Khidr (as), who said "Do not ask me about anything until I myself explain it to you."

Don't rush things. When the time is right, everything will open up and things will become clear. Allah says, "I will show you my signs, so don't rush me."

Do not ask questions too early. Have certainty that the only way you will reach Paradise is by walking on the path of Truth (through actions). Allah says, "Have they not travelled through the land so that they may see...?"

MY DEAR CHILD

I swear by Allah! If you walk the path (of truth) you will see the most astonishing things at every stop. work your soul hard, because the core aspect of this field is to work your soul hard, just like Zunnoon Misri (rh) said to one of his students: "If you have the ability to work your soul hard, then join us Sufis, if not, then don't bother busying yourself with the sham practices of the (false) Sufis."

MY DEAR CHILD

I'm going to give you 8 pieces of advice. Take them from me, so that your knowledge does not become a litigant against you on the Day of Judgement. There are 4 things for you to do, and 4 things for you to avoid.

The 4 you must leave are:

1) As far as possible, avoid engaging in debates with people. There are many risks associated with it, and the harm is far greater than the benefit. Debates and argumentation are the root cause of every rotten characteristic, like showing off, jealousy, arrogance, spite, hostility, pride and so on.

   Admittedly, if there is an issue between you and another person or group of people, and your aim and intention is to clear things up and ensure that no one is unfairly treated, then such discussion and debate is acceptable.

   However, there are 2 ways to identify such a noble intention:
   A)   you are unconcerned as to whether you say the truth, or someone else says it.
   B)   You prefer to have the conversation in private, rather than in public.

   Listen carefully! I am going to going to explain something very important to you:

   Asking questions about the problems that are troubling is equivalent to asking a doctor about an internal illness. The doctor's answer is aimed at curing that illness.

   You must understand that ignorant people are the ones with internal illness. The Scholars are their doctors.

A scholar who is not fully competent will be unable to provide good treatment. But even a competent scholar cannot heal every patient – he can only heal those patients who are willing to take the medication and accept the advice given.

Also, if the illness is a long-term illness, or one that does not respond to treatment, then treatment will be futile. Thus, a competent doctor will simply say, "This illness cannot be treated, so there is no point looking for treatment," because to attempt to heal such a person is futile.

Similarly, you must understand that the people who have this disease of ignorance fall into 4 categories.

One CAN be treated, but the other 3 cannot be treated

a)   The 1st one who cannot be treated is the one who questions and challenges due to jealousy and hatred. Every time you give him an excellent, clear and eloquent answer, it only makes him even more angry and jealous. The method of dealing with such an individual is to not bother answering him.

As the poet says:
> Every opposition can be removed
> Except the opposition of the jealous one

Thus, it is best if you turn away from him and leave him be. This is according to what Allah commands in the Quran, "So turn away from those who shun our remembrance and want only the life of this world."

The jealous one, with every word and action of his, is setting fire to his field of good deeds, and is totally unaware of it. The Prophet (saw) has said: "Jealousy eats away at good deeds, like fire eats away at dry wood."

b)   The 2nd person who cannot be treated is the one who is inherently foolish, for the foolish one cannot ever be treated. Isa (as) is reported to have said, "I am able to cause the dead to rise, but unable to treat a foolish person."

Such a person is one who engages in study for a tiny amount of time, and he learns a few bits about the secular and sacred sciences, then, due to his foolishness, he starts to question and challenge those expert scholars who have spent their whole lives learning and practicing these secular and sacred sciences. This fool has little understanding, and he thinks the things he finds challenging are also challenging to this expert scholar. When such an individual is not even able to understand this much, it is obvious that his questioning is grounded on foolishness.

Thus, it is better not to answer him, because the best way to answer a fool is not to answer him at all.

c)   The 3rd person who cannot be treated is one who is looking for guidance but who struggles. Whenever he fails to understand something that the seniors have said, he understands it is due to his lack of comprehension. He asks questions, as he wants to learn and benefit, but due to his simple nature, he is unable to comprehend the meanings of the answers.

It is best not to answer him too, because the Prophet (saw) has said, "We – as prophets – have been commanded to speak to the people according to their levels of understanding."

d)   As for the 4th person – he is the one who CAN be treated. He is looking for guidance, is intelligent, and understands well. He is not overly jealous or angry, and does not have an obsessive love for fulfilling his desires, or for fame or wealth. He is a seeker of the straight path, and his questions and challenges are not borne out of jealousy, stubbornness or to test the knowledge of others.

Such a person's ignorance CAN be treated, so it is permissible to spend time answering his questions; rather, it is your duty to spend your time answering him.

2)   The 2nd thing you must avoid is being an advisor (*wa'az*) or public speaker (*tadhkeer*). The harm is huge. If you insist on being a public advisor or speaker, you must act upon what you are going to say first, and then advise the public.

Think about what was said to Isa (as): "O son of Mary! Advise yourself. If you heed the advice, THEN advise the public. If you don't heed it, then be embarrassed before your Lord."

If you are forced into this, then ensure you avoid 2 things:
a)   Don't fill up your speech with flowery language, vague references, questionable stories, and useless bits of poetry, because Allah becomes angry with those people who put on false appearances.

When someone is overly false, it shows that the person has a poor character and is heedless (of Allah) in his heart.

What is the aim of *tadhkeer*, or reminding the people?

The aim is to remind Allah's slave of the Fire in the life hereafter, and to make him aware of how he lacks in his worship of the creator. The aim is to make him reflect on his past and have remorse at the time he wasted away in frivolous activities. The aim is to make him think about the different stages that are yet to come: Will he be able to safeguard his faith at the end of his life? What will his condition be when the angel of death comes to take him? Will be able to correctly answer the questions of the two grave-angels, Munkar and Nakeer? Will he be in a good state on the Day of Judgement, and on the plains of resurrection? Will he be able to cross the Siraat bridge safely, or will topple off it into the Fire of Hell?

The mention of all these things should remain in the listener's mind, and make him concerned and uncomfortable (about his current lifestyle). Thus, the kindling of these fires, the tears shed at the thought of these future trials is called *tadhkeer*, or reminding the people.

Directing people's attention to these things, and alerting them to their negligence and time-wasting, and helping them to see their own faults so that the congregation may feel the heat of these flames, and knowledge of these future difficulties may spur him to, as far as possible, make up for the losses of his past years and may cause him to grieve at the all the days he spent in disobedience to Allah.

A speech with all these characteristics in it, given in this way, is what is called a *wa'az* or advisory speech.

If you saw that a flood of water was headed towards someone's house, and he and his family were in the house, you would cry out, "Danger! Danger! Flee from the flood!"

In such circumstances, would you feel the need to inform your neighbour of the danger with complex language, jovial phrases and indirect speech? NO! you wouldn't ever do that.

The situation is the same for a person preaching to the congregation – he must avoid such flowery language.

b)   The 2nd thing to avoid in your speeches is that the aim of your speech mustn't be that people are captivated by your speech and cries of "Allahu Akbar" ring out, or people swoon and pass out at your words, or tear their clothes out of spiritual ecstasy, or that people say, "that was a great speech." This is because having such aims indicates a preference for the world, which is caused by being ignorant of the truth.

Rather, the aim of your speech should be direct people's focus away from the world and towards the hereafter, from sin to obedience, form greed for wealth to indifference to wealth, from being stingy to being generous, from doubt to certainty, from being ill-informed to being well-informed, and from being fooled by the world, to having total awareness of Allah.

So make them crave the life hereafter, and make them loath this worldly life, and teach them how to worship Allah and teach them abstinence. This is because people are pre-disposed to turning away from matters of the shariah and rushing towards those things that Allah is unhappy with, and adopt for themselves lowly characteristics.

So make them feel in awe of Allah, and warn them of and make them aware of the impending terrors they are to face. Their internal state may consequently change, and their external acts may transform for the good. They may start showing a desire and want to obey Allah and stop committing sin.

THIS is how you should preach to and advise the people.

Every advisory speech that is not like this, is problematic for both the speaker and the listener. It has even been said that such speeches are Jinni and Satanic speeches, that take the people away from the straight part and towards destruction.

Thus, the people must flee from such speeches because the damage such a speaker causes to their religiosity, even a devil cannot cause such damage.

Whoever has authority and power must remove such a speaker from the pulpits of the Muslims, and must stop him from what he is doing, because even this is included in the commands to order and encourage what is good, and to stop and discourage what is evil.

3) The 3rd thing you must avoid is: spending time with the leaders and sultans. You must not even look at them, because paying attention to them, sitting in their gatherings, and hanging around with them is a terrible trial. If you fall into this, then ensure you do not praise and celebrate them, because Allah becomes angry when a sinful and oppressive person is praised. As for those people who pray for the long life of an oppressive ruler - they are effectively happy with Allah being disobeyed on the earth.

4) The 4th thing you must avoid is: you must not accepts gifts and donations from people in power, even if you know the gift comes from Halal sources, because the desire for gifts from them will spoil your religiosity. You will end up flattering them, softening your stance towards them, and providing indirect support for their oppression. All of these will cause your religiosity to be weakened.

The very least that will happen is that once you have accepted their gifts, and benefitted from their worldly property, you will start to love them, and whenever you love someone, you will undoubtedly want them to have a long life and remain for longer, but by wanting an oppressive leader to remain in place, you are indirectly in favour of the public being harmed – and in favour of corruption in the world.

Is there anything else that can be more harmful to a person's religion and life hereafter than this?

Beware that you are not tempted by the devil, and by the opinions of people who say that it is better for you to take money from those in power, and then distribute it amongst the poor, because those in power are squandering that money in sin and disobedience, whereas you are spending that same money on the weak people, and your spending is better than theirs. The cursed devil has succeeded in destroying many wise people with this whisper of his.

The harms caused by this are many, and I have mentioned them in *Ihya Uloom Ad-deen* so refer to that for more details.

As for the 4 things you must do:

1) Make your relationship with Allah a positive one, such that if your employee were to have a similar relationship with you, you would be happy with him – not upset or angry with him.

   All the things you would be unhappy with your imaginary employee doing, those same things Allah, your real lord and master, would be unhappy with too.

2) Treat the people like you want to be treated, because the faith of a believer cannot be complete until he loves for the rest of the people what he loves for himself.

3) When you learn something new or revise something old, the thing you are studying should be beneficial for your heart and purify your soul. Imagine you only had a week left to live – you wouldn't spend your time studying complex legal matters, debates, principles, logic and other such subjects, because you know that these branches of knowledge will not enrich you in any way, and will instead distract you from reflecting on the state of your heart, and on realising the state of your soul. You will disconnect yourself from the world, purify your soul from negative characteristics, and engage yourself in loving Allah and in his worship, and attempt to imbibe within yourself positive characteristics.

   Remember: Not a single day or night passes, except that that day or night could possibly be your last.

MY DEAR CHILD

Listen to what else I have to say – and think about it until you are able to identify a path to salvation.

If you were to learn that the Sultan would be coming to visit you in a week, you would no doubt spend the intervening period repairing, cleaning and beautifying everything that the Sultan may end up seeing – your clothes, your body, your house, your furniture etc.

Now think about what I am hinting towards, for you are an intelligent man, and a single statement suffices for the wise one. The Prophet (saw) said, **"Allah is not interested in your body or your deeds – he is interested in your heart and your motives."**

If you want to learn more about the states of the soul, then look at my book *"Ihya uloom ad-deen"* and some of my other works. Such knowledge is an individual obligation – what every person must do – and everything else - except for that limited knowledge that would allow a person to complete the obligations Allah has placed on him - is a collective responsibility. May Allah grant you the ability to achieve this understanding of the states of the soul.

4)   Do not store up more than a year's worth of provision, which is what the Prophet (saw) used to do for some of his family members. He would pray: **"O Allah! Grant the family of Muhammad sufficient provisions."**

The Prophet (saw) didn't keep this much provision for all his family members, but only for those he felt were not as strong (in faith). As for those who had full trust in Allah, he would only keep food enough for a day or less than a day.

MY DEAR CHILD

I have written in this letter the answers to your questions. You should now act upon what I have said, and do not forget to pray for me in your pious supplications.

As for the supplication your requested from me, you will find them in the books of Sahih hadiths.

Make the following supplication in your free time, especially after the compulsory prayers:

"O Allah! O necessarily existent one! O giver of goodness and bounty! Shine upon us the lights of your mercy, and make it easy for us to fully appreciate you, Glorified are you! The only knowledge we have is the knowledge you have given us, and the only knowledge we have of you is what what you have revealed to us – you are the all-knowing, all-wise.

"O Allah! I ask you for bountiful blessings, for permanent chastity, for all-encompassing mercy, and constant good. I ask you for a good health, a comfortable lifestyle, a long life full of good happenings, an abundance of your favours, and for your blessings at every turn. I ask you for your sweetest grace, your transformative kindness, and your complete and total forgiveness.

"O Allah! Be our friend, not our foe! Let us die in a positive state and make our hopes and wishes a reality, giving us more than we wish for. Let our days and nights be days and nights of comfort and ease, and when we return to you and reach the end of our life, let us be enveloped in your mercy.

"O Allah! Pour your torrential forgiveness over our sins, and bless us by mending our faults. Make Allah-consciousness our provision, and let us work hard to spread your religion. Let our reliance and trust be upon you alone, and let us always do what pleases you.

"O Allah! Keep us firmly on the straight path, and grant us entry into our permanent home (of Paradise). Whilst we are in the world, protects us from those actions that will undoubtedly be a source of regret in the hereafter. Lighten the burden of our sins, and let us live the lives of the pious. Be sufficient for us, and divert the evil of the evildoers and the plots of the plotters away from us. Free us, and our fathers, our mothers, brothers (and our sisters) from the fire – do all this through your mercy, for you are the most powerful, the most forgiving, the most generous, the greatest concealer of faults, the most tolerant. You are the controller, O Allah! O Allah! Do all this through your mercy, O most merciful one!"

== the book is now complete ==

بسم الله الرحمن الرحيم الحمد لله رب العالمين والعاقبة للمتقين والصلاة والسلام على سيدنا ومولانا محمد رسول الله (صلي الله عليه وسلم) وآله وصحبه أجمعين.

إعلم أيها الولد والمحب العزيز ـ أطال الله بقاك بطاعته وسلك بك سبيل أحبائه: أن منشور النصيحة يكتب من معدن الرسالة. إن كان قد بلغك منه نصيحة فأي حاجة لك في نصيحتي وإن لم يبلغك فقل لي: ماذا حصلت في هذه السنين الماضية ؟

أيها الولد: من جملة ما نصح به رسول الله (صلى الله عليه وسلم) امته قوله عليه الصلاة والسلام : "علامة إعراض الله تعالي عن العبد اشتغاله بما لا يعنيه وإن أمرا ذهبت ساعة من عمره في غير ما خلق له من العبادة لجدير أن تطول عليه حسرته ومن جاوز الأربعين ولم يغلب خيره على شره فليتجهز إلى النار".

وفي هذه النصيحة كفاية لأهل العلم.

أيها الولد: النصيحة سهلة والمشكل قبولها لأنها في مذاق متبعي الهوى مرة. إذ المناهي محبوبة في قلوبهم وعلى الخصوص لمن طالب العلم الرسمي ومشتغلا في فضل النفس ومناقب الدنيا فإنه يحسب أن العلم المجرد له سيكون نجاته وخلاصه فيه وأنه مستغن عن العمل وهذا اعتقاد الفلاسفة.

سبحان الله العظيم ! لا يعلم هذا المغرور أنه حين حصل العلم إذا لم يعمل به تكون الحجة عليه آكد كما قال رسول الله (صلى الله عليه وسلم): "أشد الناس عذابا يوم القيامة عالم لا ينفعه الله بعلمه". وروي أن الجنيد (قدِس الله سره) 'روي في المنام بعد موته فقيل له: ما الخبر يا أبا القاسم ؟ قال: "طاحت تلك

العبارات وفنيت تلك الإشارات وما نفعنا إلا 'ركيعات ركعناها في جوف الليل".

أيها الولد: لا تكون من الأعمال مفلسا ولا من الأحوال خاليا وتيقن أن العلم المجرد لا يأخذ باليد. مثاله لو كان على رجل في برية عشرة أسياف هندية مع أسلحة اخري وكان الرجل شجاعا وأهل حرب فحمل عليه أسد عظيم مهيب فما ظنك؟ هل تدفع الأسلحة شره عنه بلا استعمالها وضربها؟ ومن المعلوم أنها لا تدفع إلا بالتحريك والضرب. فكذا لو قرأ رجل مائة ألف مسالة علمية وتعلمها ولم يعمل بها لا تفيده إلا بالعمل. ومثله ايضا لو كان لرجل حرارة ومرض صفراوي يكون علاجه بالسكنجبين والكشكاب فلا يحصل (بيت باللسان   البرء إلا باستعمالهما.

الفارسي) كرمى دو هزار رطل همى بيمائيتامى نخورى نباشدت شيدائي(1)

ولو قرأت العلم مائة سنة وجمعت ألف كتاب لا تكون مستعدا لرحمة الله تعالى إلا بالعمل لقوله سبحانه وتعالى "وأن ليس للإنسان إلا ماسعى" "فمن كان يرجو لقاء ربه فليعمل عملا صالحا" "جزاء بما كانوا يكسبون" "إن الذين آمنوا وعملوا الصالحات كانت لهم جنات الفردوس نزلا خالدين فيها لا يبغون عنها حولا" "فخلف من بعدهم خلف أضاعوا الصلوة واتبعوا الشهوات فسوف يلقون غيا إلا من تاب وآمن وعمل صالحا فأولئك يدخلون الجنة ولا يظلمون شيئا. وما تقول في هذا الحديث: "بني الإسلام على خمس: شهادة أن لا اله إلا الله وأن محمدا رسول الله وإقام الصلاة وإيتاء الزكاة وصوم رمضان وحج البيت لمن استطاع إليه سبيلا". والإيمان قول باللسان وتصديق بالجنان وعمل بالأركان ودليل الأعمال أكثر من أن يحصي وإن كان العبد يبلغ الجنة بفضل الله تعالي وكرمه.

لكن بعد أن يستعد بطاعته وعبادته لأن "رحمة الله قريب من المحسنين". ولو قيل أيضا: يبلغ بمجرد الإيمان قلنا: نعم ولكن متى يبلغ؟ وكم من عقبة كوود يقطعها إلى أن يصل؟ فأول تلك العقبات عقبة الإيمان وأنه هل يسلم من سلب الإيمان أم لا؟ وإذا وصل هل يكون خائبا مفلسا؟ وقال الحسن البصري (رضي الله عنه): "يقول الله تعالى لعباده يوم القيامة: ادخلوا يا عباديالجنة برحمتي واقتسموها بأعمالكم".

أيها الولد: مالم تعمل لم تجد الأجر. حكي أن رجلا من بني إسرائيل عبد الله تعالى سبعين سنة فأراد الله تعالى أن يجلوه على الملائكة فأرسل الله إليه ملكا يخبره أنه مع تلك العبادة لا يليق به دخول الجنة فلما بلغه قال العابد: نحن خلقنا للعبادة فينبغي لنا أن نعبده. فلما رجع الملك قال: إلهي أنت أعلم بما قال. فقال الله تعالى: "إذا هو لم يعرض عن عبادتنا فنحن مع الكرام لا نعرض عنه إشهدوا يا ملائكتى أني قد غفرت له". وقال سيدنا رسول الله (صلى الله عليه وسلم): "حاسبوا أنفسكم قبل أن تحاسبوا وزنوا أعمالكم قبل أن توزنوا" وقال سيدنا علي (رضي الله عنه): "من ظن أنه بدون الجهد بصل فهو متمن ومن ظن أنه ببذل الجهد يصل فهو مستغن" , وقال سيدنا الحسن (رضي الله عنه) : "طلب الجنة بلاعمل ذنب من الذنوب" وقال: "علامةالحقيقة ترك ملاحظة العمل لا ترك العمل" وقال سيدنا رسول الله (صلى الله عليه وسلم): "الكيس من دان نفسه وعمل لما بعد الموت والأحمق من اتبع هواه و تمني على الله تعالى الأماني".

أيها الولد: كم من ليال أحييتها بتكرار العلم ومطالعة الكتب وحرمت علي نفسك النوم؟ لا أعلم ما كان الباعث فيه. إن كان

نيل عرض الدنيا وجذب حطامها وتحصيل مناصبها والمباهاة علي الأقران والأمثال فويل لك ثم ويل لك. وإن كان قصدك فيه إحياء شريعة النبي (صلى الله عليه وسلم) وتهذيب أخلاقك وكسر النفس الأمارة بالسوء فطوبي لك ثم طوبي لك. ولقد صدق من قال شعرا : سهر العيون لغير وجهك ضائعوبكاؤهن لغير فقدك باطل

أيها الولد: عش ما شئت فإنك ميت وأحبب ما شئت فإنك مفارقه واعمل ما شئت فإنك مجزي به.

أيها الولد أي شيء حاصل لك من تحصيل علم الكلام والخلاف والطب والدواوين والأشعار والنجوم والعروض والنحو والتصريفغير تضيع العمر بخلاف ذي الجلال. إني رأيت في إنجيل سيدنا عيسى (عليه الصلاة والسلام): "من ساعة أن يوضع الميت علي الجنازة إلي أن يوضع على شفير القبر يسأل الله تعالي بعظمته منه أربعين سؤالا. أولها يقول: عبدي طهرت منظر الخلق سنين وما طهرت منظري ساعة. وكل يوم ينظر في قلبك يقول: ما تصنع لغيري وأنت محفوف بخيري. أما أنت فأصم لا تسمع".

أيها الولد: العلم بلا عمل جنون والعمل بلا علم لا يكون. واعلم أن العلم الذي لا يبعدك اليوم عن المعاصي ولا يحملك على الطاعة لن يبعدك غدا عن نار جهنم وإذا لم تعمل بعلمك اليوم ولم تدارك الأيام الماضية تقول غدا يوم القيامة: "فأرجعنا نعمل صالحا". فيقال: "يا أحمق أنت من هناك تجيء".

أيها الولد: اجعل الهمة في الروح والهزيمة في النفس والموت في البدن لانمنزلك القبر وأهل المقابر ينتظرونك في كل لحظة

متي تصل إليهم. إياك إياك أنتصل إليهم بلا زاد. قال سيدنا أبو بكر الصديق (رضي الله عنه): "هذه الأجساد قفص الطيور أو إصطبل الدواب فتفكر في نفسك: من أيهما أنت؟ إن كنت من الطيور العلوية فحين تسمع طنين طبل ارجعي إلي ربك تطير صاعدا إلي أن تقعد في أعالي بروج الجنان". وكما قال سيدنا رسول الله (صلي الله عليه وسلم) : "اهتز عرش الرحمن من موت سعد بن معاذ (رضي الله عنه)" والعياذ بالله إن كنت من الدواب كما قال الله تعالي: "أولئك كالأنعام بل هم أضل" فلا تأمن انتقالك من زاوية الدار إلي هاوية النار. وروي أن سيدنا الحسن البصري (رحمه الله تعالي) أعطي شربة ماء بارد فاخذ القدح وغشي عليه وسقط من يده فلما أفاق قيل: مالك يا أبا سعيد؟ قال: ذكرت أمنية أهل النار حين يقولون لأهل الجنة: "أن أفيضوا علينا من الماء أو مما رزقكم الله".

أيها الولد: لو كان العلم المجرد كافيا لك ولا تحتاج إلي عمل سواه لكان نداء"هل من سائل؟ هل من مستغفر؟ هل من منتائب؟" ضائعا بلا فائدة. وروي أن جماعة من الصحابة (رضوان الله عليهم اجمعين) ذكروا سيدنا عبد الله بن عمر (رضي الله عنهما) عند سيدنا رسول الله (صلي الله عليه وسلم) , فقال: "نعم الرجل هو لو كان يصلي بالليل". وقال عليه الصلاة والسلام لرجل من أصحابه: "يا فلان لا تكثر النوم بالليل فان كثرة النوم بالليل يدع صاحبه فقيرا يوم القيامة".

أيها الولد "ومن الليل فتهجد به نافلة لك" أمر "وبالأسحار هم يستغفرون" شكر "والمستغفرون بالأسحار" ذكر. قال عليه الصلاة والسلام: "ثلاثة أصوات يحبها الله تعالي: صوت الديك وصوت الذي يقرأ القرآن وصوت المستغفرين بالأسحار" وقال

سيدنا سفيان الثوري (رحمة الله تعالى عليه): "إن الله تبارك وتعالى خلق ريحا تهب بالأسحار تحمل الأذكار والاستغفار إلي الملك الجبار" وقال أيضا: "إذا كان أول الليل ينادي مناد من تحت العرش: ألآ ليقمالعابدون فيقومون ويصلون ما شاء الله ثم ينادي مناد في شطر الليل: ألا ليقم القانتون فيقومون ويصلون إلي السحر فإذا كان السحر نادي مناد: ألا ليقم المستغفرون و يستغفرون فإذا طلع الفجر نادي مناد: ألا ليقم الغافلون فيقومون من فرشهم كالموتى نشروا من قبورهم".

أيها الولد: روي في وصايا لقمان الحكيم لابنه أنه قال: "يابني لا يكنن الديك أكيس منك ينادي بالأسحار وأنت نائم". ولقد أحسن من قال شعراً: على   لقد هتفت في جنح ليل حمامةفنن وهنا وأني لنائم لما كذبت وبيت الله لو كنت عاشقاسبقتني بالبكاء الحمائموأزعم أني هائم ذو صبابة لربي فلا أبكي وتبكي البهائم

أيها الولد: خلاصة العلم أن تعلم الطاعة والعبادة ما هي. أعلم أن الطاعة والعبادة متابعة الشارع في الأوامروالنواهي بالقول والفعل. يعني: كل ما تقولوتفعل وتترك يكون بإقتداء الشرع كما لو صمت يوم العيد وأيام التشريق تكون عاصيا أو صليت في ثوب مغصوب وإن كانت صورة عبادة تأثم.

أيها الولد: ينبغي لك أن يكون قولك وفعلك موافقا للشرع إذ العلم والعمل بلا إقتداء الشرع ضلالة وينبغي لك ألا تغتر بالشطح وطامات الصوفية لأن سلوك هذا الطريق يكون بالمجاهدة وقطع شهوة النفس وقتل هواها بسيف الرياضة لا بالطامات والترهات. وأعلم أن اللسان المطلق والقلب المطبق

المملوء بالغفلة والشهوة وعلامة الشقاوة فإذا لم تقتل النفس بصدق المجاهدة فلن يحيا قلبك بأنوار المعرفة. وأعلم أن بعض مسائلك التي سألتني عنها لا يستقيم جوابها بالكتابة والقول. إن تبلغ تلك الحالة تعرف ما هي وإلا فعلمها من المستحيلات لأنها ذوقية وكل ما يكون ذوقيا لا يستقيم وصفه بالقول كحلاوة الحلو ومرارة المر لا تعرف إلا بالذوق. كماحكي أن عنينا (غبيا) كتب إلي صاحب له أن عرفني لذة المجامعة كيف تكون. فكتب له في جوابه: يا فلان إني كنت حسبتك عنينا فقط. والآن عرفت أنك عنين وأحمق. لأن هذه اللذة ذوقية إن تصل إليها تعرف وإلا لا يستقيم وصفها بالقول والكتابة.

أيها الولد: بعض مسائلك من هذا القبيل وأما البعض الذي يستقيم له الجواب فقد ذكرناه في "إحياء العلوم" و غيره. ونذكر هاهنا نبدأ منه ونشير إليه فنقول: قد وجب علي السالك أربعة أمور:**الأمر الأول:** اعتقاد صحيح لا يكون فيه بدعة. **الأمر الثاني:** توبة نصوح لا يرجع بعدها إلي الزلة. **الأمر الثالث:** استرضاء الخصوم حتى لا يبقي لأحد عليك حق. **الأمر الرابع:** تحصيل علم الشريعة قدرما تؤدي به أوامر الله تعالى ثم من العلومالأخرى ما تكون به النجاة. حكي أن سيدنا الشبلي (رحمه الله) خدم أربعمائة استاذ وقال: قرأت أربعة آلاف حديث ثم اخترت منها حديثا واحدا وعملت به وخليت ما سواه لأني تأملته فوجدت خلاصي ونجاتي فيه وكان علم الأولين والآخرين كله مندرجا فيه فاكتفيت به وذلك أن سيدنا رسول الله (صلي الله عليه وسلم) قال لبعض أصحابه: "إعمل لدنياك بقدر مقامك فيها واعمل لأخرتك بقدر بقائك فيها واعمل لله بقدر حاجتك إليه واعمل للنار بقدر صبرك عليها".

أيها الولد: إذا علمت هذا الحديث لا حاجة إلي العلم الكثير. وتأمل في حكايات اخري وذلك أن سيدنا حاتم الأصم (رحمه الله) كان من أصحاب سيدنا الشقيق البلخي (رحمة الله) فسأله يوما: صاحبتني منذ ثلاثين سنة ما حصلت فيها؟ قال: حصلتعلى ثماني فوائد من العلم وهي تكفيني منهلأني أرجو خلاصي ونجاتي فيها. فقالشقيق: ما هي؟ قال حاتم الأصم: **الفائدة الأولى:** أني نظرت إلي الخلق فرأيت لكل منهم محبوبا ومعشوقا يحبه ويعشقه وبعض ذلك المحبوب يصاحبه إلي مرض الموت وبعضه إلي شفير القبر ثم يرجع كله ويتركه فريدا وحيدا ولا يدخل معه في قبره منهم أحد فتفكرت وقلت: أفضل محبوب المرء ما يدخل في قبره ويوانسه فيه فما وجدت غير الأعمال الصالحة فأخذتها محبوبا لي لتكون سراجا لي في قبري وتوانسني فيه ولا تتركني فريدا. **الفائدة الثانية:** أني رأيت الخلق يقتدون بأهوائهم ويبادرون إلي مرادات أنفسهم فتأملت قوله تعالي: "وأما من خاف مقام ربه ونهي النفس عن الهوى فإن الجنة هي المأوي" وتيقنت أن القرآن حق وصدق فبادرت إلي خلاف نفسي وتشمرت لمجاهدتها ومنعها عن هواها حتى ارتاضت لطاعة الله سبحانه وتعالي وانقادت. **الفائدة الثالثة:** أني رأيت كل واحد من الناس يسعى في جمع حطام الدنيا ثم يمسكه قابضا يده عليه فتأملت في قوله تعالي: "ما عندكم ينفذ وما عند الله باق". فبذلت محصولي من الدنيا لوجه الله تعالي ففرقته بين المساكين ليكون ذخرا لي عند الله تعالي. **الفائدة الرابعة:** أني رأيت بعض الخلق ظن شرفه وعزه في كثرة الأقوام والعشائر فاغتر بهم وزعم آخرون أنه في ثروة الأموال وكثرة الأولاد فافتخروا بها وحسب بعضهم الشرف والعز في

غصب أموال الناس وظلمهم وسفك دمائهم واعتقدت طائفة أنه في إتلاف المال إسرافه وتبذيره وتأملت في قوله تعالى: "إن أكرمكم عند الله اتقاكم". فاخترت التقوى واعتقدت أن القرآن حق صادق وظنهم وحسبانهم كلها باطل زائل. **الفائدة الخامسة**: أني رأيت الناس يذم بعضهم بعضا ويغتاب بعضهم بعضا فوجدت ذلك من الحسد في المال والجاه والعلم فتأملت في قوله تعالى: "نحن قسمنا بينهم معيشتهم في الحياة الدنيا". فعلمت أن القسمة كانت من الله تعالى في الأزل فما حسدت أحدا ورضيت بقسمة الله تعالى. **الفائدة السادسة**: أني رأيت الناس يعادي بعضهم لغرض وسبب فتأملت قوله تعالى: "إن الشيطان لكم عدو فاتخذوه عدوا". فعلمت أنه لا تجوز عداوة أحد غير الشيطان. **الفائدة السابعة**: أني رأيت كل أحد يسعى بجد ويجتهد بمبالغة لطلب القوت والمعاش بحيث يقع به في شبهة وحرام ويذل نفسه وينقص قدره فتأملت في قوله تعالى: "وما من دابة في الأرض إلا على الله رزقها". فعلمت أن رزقي على الله تعالى وقد ضمنه فاشتغلت بعبادته وقطعت طمعي عمن سواه. **الفائدة الثامنة**: أني رأيت كل واحد معتمدا على شئ مخلوق: بعضهم إلى الدينار والدرهم وبعضهم إلى المال والملك وبعضهم إلى الحرفة والصناعة وبعضهم إلى مخلوق مثله فتأملت في قوله تعالى: "ومن يتوكل على الله فهو حسبه إن الله بالغ أمره قد جعل الله لكل شئ قدرا". فتوكلت على الله فهو حسبي ونعم الوكيل. فقال سيدنا شقيق (رحمه الله): وفقك الله تعالى إني قد نظرت التوراة والزبور والإنجيل والفرقان فوجدت الكتب الأربعة تدور على هذه الفوائد الثمانية. فمن عمل بها كان عاملا بهذه الكتب الأربعة.

أيها الولد: قد علمت من هاتين الحكايتين أنك لا تحتاج إلى تكثير العلم. **والآن أبين لك ما يجب على سالك سبيل الحق:** إعلم أنه ينبغي للسالك شيخ مرشد مرب ليخرج الأخلاق السيئة منه بتربيته ويجعل مكانها خلقا حسنا ومعنى التربية يشبه فعل الفلاح الذي يقلع الشوك ويخرج النباتات الأجنبية من بين الزرع ليحسن نباته ويكمل ريعه. ولا بد للسالك من شيخ يؤدبه ويرشده إلى سبيل الله تعالى لأن اللهأرسل للعباد رسولا للإرشاد إلى سبيله. فإذاارتحل صلي الله عليه وسلم فقد خلفالخلفاء في مكانه حتى يرشدوا إلى الله تعالى. وشرط الشيخ الذي يصلح أن يكون نائبا لسيدنا رسول الله (صلوات الله وسلامه عليه) أن يكون عالما ولكن لا كل عالم يصلح للخلافة. وإني أبين لك بعض علاماته على سبيل الإجمال حتى لا يدعي كل أحد أنه مرشد. فنقول: من يعرض عن حب الدنيا وحب الجاه وكان قد تابع لشخص بصير تتسلسل متابعته إلى سيد المرسلين (صلي الله عليه وسلم) وكان محسنا رياضة نفسه بقلة الأكل والقول والنوم وكثرة الصلوات والصدقة والصوم وكان بمتابعته ذلك الشيخ البصير جاعلا محاسن الأخلاق له سيرة كالصبر والصلاة والشكر والتوكل واليقين والقناعة وطمأنينة النفس والحلم والتواضع والعلم والصدق والحياء والوفاء والوقار والسكون والتأني وأمثالها. فهو إذا نور من أنوار سيدنا النبي (صلي الله عليه وسلم) يصلح للإقتداء بهولكن وجود مثله نادر أعز من الكبريت الأحمر ومن ساعدته السعادة فوجد شيخا كما ذكرنا وقبله الشيخ ينبغي أن يحترمه ظاهرا وباطنا. أما احترام الظاهر فهو ألا يجادله ولا يشتغل بالاحتجاج معه في كل مسألة وإن علم خطاه. ولا يلقي بين يديه سجادته إلا وقت أداء

الصلاة فإذا فرغ يرفعها. ولا يكثر نوافل الصلاة بحضرته. ويعمل ما يأمره الشيخ من العمل بقدر وسعه وطاقته. وأما احترام الباطن فهو أن كل ما يسمع ويقبل منه في الظاهر لا ينكره في الباطن لا فعلا ولا قولا لئلا يتسم بالنفاق. وإن لم يستطع يترك صحبته إلى أن يوافق باطنه ظاهره. ويحترز عن مجالسة صاحب السوء ليقصر ولاية شياطين الجن والإنس عن صحن قلبه فيصفي من لوث الشيطنة وعلى كل حال يختار الفقر على الغني. **ثم اعلم أن التصوف له خصلتان:** الاستقامة مع الله تعالى. والسكون عن الخلق. فمن استقام مع الله عز وجل وأحسنخلقه بالناس وعاملهم بالحلم فهو صوفي. والاستقامة أن يفدي حظ نفسه على أمر الله تعالى. وحسن الخلق مع الناس ألا تحمل الناس علي مراد نفسك بل تحمل نفسك علي مرادهم ما لم يخالفوا الشرع. **ثم إنك سألتني عن العبودية وهي ثلاثة أشياء:** محافظة أمر الشرع. الرضاء بالقضاء والقدر وقسمة الله تعالى. ترك رضاء نفسك في طلب رضاء الله تعالى. وسألتني عن التوكل وهو أن يستحكم اعتقادك بالله تعالى فيما وعد يعني تعتقد أن ما قدر لك سيصل إليك لا محالة وإن اجتهد كل من في العالم على صرفه عنك وما لم يكتب لن يصل إليك وإن ساعدك جميع العالم. وسألتني عن الإخلاص وهو أن تكون أعمالك كلها لله تعالى ولا يرتاح قلبك بمحامد الناس ولا تبالي بمذمتهم. واعلم أن الرياء يتولد من تعظيم الخلق. وعلاجه أن تراهم مسخرين تحت القدرة وتحسبهم كالجمادات في عدم قدرة إيصال الراحة والمشقة لتخلص من مراءاتهم. ومتى تحسبهم ذوي قدرة وإرادة لن يبعد عنك الرياء.

أيها الولد: والباقي من مسائلك بعضها مسطور

في مصنفاتي فاطلبه ثمة وكتابة بعضها حرام.

إعمل أنت بما تعلم لينكشف لك ما لم تعلم.

أيها الولد: بعد اليوم لا تسألني ما أشكل عليك إلا بلسان الجنان لقوله تعالى: "ولو أنهم صبروا حتى تخرج إليهم لكان خيرا لهم". واقبل نصيحة سيدنا الخضر (عليه السلام) حين قال: "فلا تسألني عن شئ حتى أحدث لك منه ذكرا". ولا تستعجل حتى تبلغ أوانه فينكشف لك وتراه لقوله تعالى "سأريكم آياتي فلا تستعجلون". فلا تسألني قبل الوقت وتيقن أنك لا تصل إلا بالسير لقوله تعالى "أو لم يسيروا فيالأرض فينظروا".

أيها الولد: بالله إن تسر تر العجائب في كل منزل وابذل روحك فإن رأس هذا الأمر بذل الروح كما قال سيدنا ذو النون المصري (رحمه الله تعالى) لأحد تلامذته: "إن قدرت علي بذل الروح فتعال وإلا فلا تشتغل بترهات الصوفية".

أيها الولد: إني أنصحك بثمانية أشياء إقبلها مني لئلا يكون علمك خصما عليك يوم القيامة. تعمل منها أربعة وتدع منها أربعة. أما الأربعة اللواتي تدع: **أولاً:** ألا تناظر أحدا في مسألة ما استطعت لأن فيها آفات كثيرة فإثمها أكبر من نفعها إذ هي منبع كل خلق ذميم كالرياء والحسد والكبر والحقد والعداوة والمباهاة وغيرها. نعم لو وقع مسألة بينك وبين شخص أو قوم وكانت إرادتك فيها أن يظهر الحق ولا يضيع جاز البحث. **لكن لتلك الإرادة علامتان: أحداهما:** ألا تفرق بين أن ينكشف الحق على لسانك أو على لسان غيرك. **والثانية:** أن يكون البحث في الخلاء أحب إليك من أن يكون في الملا. واسمع إني أذكر لك ها هنا فائدة واعلم أن السؤال عن المشكلات عرض مرض القلب إلى الطبيب والجواب له سعي لإصلاح مرضه. واعلم أن

الجاهلين المرضي قلوبهم والعلماء الأطباء والعالم الناقص لا يحسن المعالجة والعالم الكامل لا يعالج كل مريض بل يعالج من يرجو قبول المعالجة والصلاح وإذا كانت العلة مزمنة أو عقيما لا تقبل العلاج فحذاقة الطبيب فيه أن يقول هذا لا يقبل العلاج فلا تشتغل فيه بمداواته لأن فيه تضييع العمر. **ثم اعلم أن مرض الجهل على أربعة أنواع:** يقبل العلاج والباقي لا يقبل. أما الذي لا يقبل العلاج كان اعتراضه عن حسده وبغضه فكلما تجيبه بأحسن الجواب وأفصحه وأوضحه فلا يزيد له ذلك إلا بغضا وعداوة وحسدا فالطريق ألا تشتغل بجوابه فقد قيل: كل العداوة قد إلا عداوة من عاداك عن ترجي إزالتها حسد فينبغي أن تعرض عنه وتتركه مع مرضه. قال الله تعالى: "فأعرض عمن تولى عن ذكرنا ولم يرد إلا الحياة الدنيا". والحسود بكل ما يقول ويفعل يوقد النار في زرع عمله كما قال النبي (عليه الصلاة والسلام): "الحسد يأكل الحسنات كما تأكل النار الحطب". أن تكون علته من الحماقة وهو أيضا لا يقبل العلاج. كما قال عيسى (عليه السلام): "إني ما عجزت عن إحياء الموتى وقد عجزت عن معالجة الأحمق". وذلك رجل يشتغل بطلب العلم زمنا قليلا ويتعلم شيئا من العلم العقلي والشرعي فيسأل ويعترض من حماقته على العالم الكبير الذي مضى عمره في العلوم العقلية والشرعية وهذا الأحمق لا يعلم ويظن أن ما أشكل عليه هو ايضا مشكل على العالم الكبير. فإذا لم يعلم هذا القدر يكون سؤاله من الحماقة. فينبغي ألا تشتغل بجوابه. أن يكون مسترشدا. وكل ما لا يفهم من كلام الأكابر يحمل على قصور فهمه وكان سؤاله للاستفادة لكن يكون بليدا لا يدرك الحقائق فلا ينبغي الاشتغال بجوابه ايضا كما قال رسول الله (صلي الله

عليه وسلم): "نحن معاشر الأنبياء امرنا أن نكلم الناس على قدر عقولهم". أما المرض الذي يقبل العلاج فهو أن يكون مسترشدا عاقلا. فهما لا يكون مغلوب الحسد والغضب وحب الشهرة والجاه والمال ويكون طالب الطريق المستقيم ولم يمن سؤاله واعتراضه عن حسد وتعنت وامتحان. وهذا يقبل العلاج فيجوز أن تشتغل بجواب سؤاله بل يجب عليك إجابته. **ثانياً:** مما تدع هو أن تحذر من أن تكون واعظا ومذكرا لأن فيه آفة كثيرة إلا أن تعمل بما تقول أولا ثم تعظ به الناس. فتفكر فيما قيل لعيسى (عليه السلام): "يا ابن مريم عظ نفسك فإن اتعظت فعظ الناسوإلا فاستح من ربك". **وإن ابتليت بهذا العمل فاحترز عن خصلتين: (1) الخصلة الأولى:** عن التكلف في الكلام بالعبارات والإشارات والطامات والأبيات والأشعار لأن الله تعالى يبغض المتكلفين والمتكلف المتجاوز عن الحد يدل على خراب الباطن وغفلة القلب ومعنى التذكير أن يذكر العبد نار الآخرة وتقصير نفسه في خدمة الخالق ويتفكر في عمره الماضي الذي أفناه فيما لا يعينه ويتفكر فيما بين يديه من العقبات من عدم سلامة الإيمان في الخاتمة وكيفية حاله في قبض ملك الموت وهل يقدر على جواب منكر ونكير ويهتم بحاله في القيامة ومواقفها وهل يعبر عن الصراط سالما أم يقع في الهاوية؟ ويستمر ذكر هذه الأشياء في قلبه فيزعجه عن قراره. فغليان هذه النيران ونوحة هذه المصائب يسمى تذكيرا. وإعلام الخلق وإطلاعهم على هذه الأشياء وتنبيههم على تقصيرهم وتفريطهم وتبصيرهم بعيوب أنفسهم لتمس حرارة هذه النيران أهل المجلس وتجزعهم تلك المصائب ليتداركوا العمر الماضي بقدر الطاقة ويتحسروا على الأيام الخالية في غير طاعة الله تعالى:

هذه الجملة على هذا الطريق تسمى وعظا. كما لو رأيت أن السيل قد هجم على دار أحد وكان هو وأهله فيها فتقول: الحذر الحذر فروا من السيل. وهل يشتهي قلبك في هذه الحالة أن تخبر صاحب الدار خبرك بتكلف العبارات والنكت والإشارات فلا تشتهي البتة فكذلك حال الواعظ فينبغي أن يتجنبها. **(2) والخصلة الثانية**: ألا تكون همتك في وعظك أن ينعر الخلق في مجلسك أو يظهروا الوجد ويشقوا الثياب ليقال: نعم المجلس هذا! لأن كله ميل للدنيا وهو يتولد من الغفلة. بل ينبغي أن يكون عزمك وهمتك أن تدعو الناس من الدنيا إلى الآخرة ومن المعصية إلى الطاعة ومن الحرص إلى الزهد ومن البخل إلى السخاء ومن الشك إلى اليقين ومن الغفلة إلى اليقظة ومن الغرور إلى التقوى وتحبب إليهم الآخرة وتبغض إليهم الدنيا وتعلمهم علم العبادة والزهد ولا تغرهم بكرم الله تعالى عز وجل ورحمته , لأن الغالب في طباعهم الزيغ عن منهج الشرع والسعي فيما لا يرضى الله تعالى به والاستعثار بالأخلاق الردية. فألق في قلوبهم الرعب وروعهم وحذرهم عما يستقبلون من المخاوف لعل صفات باطنهم تتغير ومعاملة ظاهرهم تتبدل ويظهر الحرص والرغبة في الطاعة والرجوع عن المعصية. وهذا طريق الوعظ والنصيحة وكل وعظ لا يكون هكذا فهو وبال على من قال وسمع بل قيل: إنه غول وشيطان يذهب بالخلق عن الطريق ويهلكهم فيجب عليهم أن يفروا منه لأن ما يفسد هذا القائل من دينهم لا يستطيع بمثله الشيطان. ومن كانت له يد وقدرة يجب عليه أن ينزله عن منابر المواعظ ويمنعه عما باشر فإنه من جملة الأمر بالمعروف والنهي عن المنكر. **ثالثاً**: مما تدع ألا تخالط الأمراء والسلاطين ولا تراهم لأن

رؤيتهم ومجالستهم ومخالطتهم آفة عظيمة ولو ابتليت بها دع عنك مدحهم وثناهم لأن الله تعالى يغضب إذا مدح الفاسق والظالم. ومن دعا لطول بقائهم فقد أحب أن يعصى الله تعالى في أرضه. **رابعاً:** مما تدع ألا تقبل شيئا من عطاء الأمراء وهداياهم وإن علمت أنها من الحلال. لأن الطمع منهم يفسد الدين لأنه يتولد منه المداهنة ومراعاة جانبهم والموافقة في ظلمهم. وهذا كله فساد في الدين وأقل مضرته أنك إذا قبلت عطاياهم وانتفعت من دنياهم أحببتهم ومن أحب أحدا يحب طول عمره وبقائه بالضرورة وفي محبة الظالم إرادة في الظلم على عباد الله تعالى وإرادة خراب العالم. فأي شيء يكون أضر من هذا للدين والعاقبة؟ وإياك إياك أنيخدعك استهواء الشياطين أو قول بعضالناس لك بأن الأفضل والأولى أن تأخذالدينار والدرهم منهم وتفرقهما بين الفقراء والمساكين فإنهم ينفقون في الفسق والمعصية وإنفاقك على ضعفاء الناس خير من إنفاقهم فإن اللعين قد قطع أعناق كثير من الناس بهذه الوسوسة وقد ذكرناه في إحياء العلوم فاطلبه ثمة. **وأما الأربعة التي ينبغي لك أن تفعلها : أولاً:** أن تجعل معاملتك مع الله تعالى بحيث لو عامل معك بها عبدك ترضى بها منه ولا يضيق خاطرك عليه ولا تغضب والذي لا ترضى لنفسك من عبدك المجازي فلا ترض أيضا لله تعالى وهو سيدك الحقيقي. **ثانياً:** كلما عملت بالناس اجعله كما ترضى لنفسك منهم لأنه لا يكمل إيمان عبد حتى يحب لسائر الناس ما يحب لنفسه. **ثالثاً:** إذا قرأت العلم أو طالعته ينبغي أن يكون علمك يصلح قلبك ويزكي نفسك كما لو علمت أن عمرك ما يبقى غير أسبوع فبالضرورة لا تشتغل فيها بعلم الفقه والأخلاق والأصول

والكلام وأمثالها لأنك تعلم أن هذه العلوم لا تغنيك. بل تشتغل بمراقبة القلب ومعرفة صفات النفس والإعراض عن علائق الدنيا وتزكي نفسك عن الأخلاق الذميمة وتشتغل بمحبة الله تعالى وعبادته والاتصاف بالأوصاف الحسنة ولا يمر على عبد يوم وليلة إلا ويمكن أن يكون موته فيه.

أيها الولد: إسمع مني كلاما آخر وتفكر فيه حتى تجد خلاصا: لو أنك أخبرت أن السلطان بعد أسبوع يجيئك زائرا فأنا أعلم أنك في تلك المدة لا تشتغل إلا بإصلاح ما علمت أن نظر السلطان سيقع عليه من الثياب والبدن والدار والفراش وغيرها والآن تفكر إلى ما أشرت به فإنك فهم والكلام الفرد يكفي الكيس قال سيدنا رسول الله (عليه الصلاة والسلام): "إن الله لا ينظر إلى صوركم ولا إلى أعمالكم ولكن ينظر إلى قلوبكم ونياتكم" وإن أردت علمأحوال القلب فانظر إلى "الإحياء" وغيرهمن مصنفاتي. وهذا العلم فرض عينوغيره فرض كفاية إلا مقدار ما يؤدى بهفرائض الله تعالى وهو يوفقك حتى تحصله. **رابعاً:** ألا تجمع من الدنيا أكثر من كفاية سنة كما كان سيدنا رسول الله (عليه الصلاة والسلام) يعد ذلك لبعض حجراته وقال: "اللهم اجعل قوت آل محمد كفافا". ولم يكن يعد ذلك لكل حجراته بل كان يعده لمن علم أن في قلبها ضعفا. وأما من كانت صاحبة يقين فما كان يعد لها أكثر من قوت يوم أو نصف.

أيها الولد: إني كتبت في هذا الفصل ملتمساتك فينبغي لك أن تعمل بها ولا تنساني فيه من أن تذكرني في صالح دعائك. وأما الدعاء الذي سألت مني فاطلبه من دعوات الصحاح وأقرأ هذا الدعاء في جميع أوقاتك خصوصا أعقاب صلواتك: "اللهم إني أسألك من النعمة تمامها ومن العصمة دوامها ومن الرحمة

شمولها ومن العافية حصولها ومن العيش أرغده ومن العمر أسعده ومن الإحسان أتمه ومن الإنعام أعمه ومن الفضل أعذبه ومن اللطف أقربه. أللهم كن لنا ولا تكن علينا. أللهم اختم بالسعادة آجالنا وحقق بالزيادة آمالنا واقرن بالعافية غدونا وآصالنا واجعل إلى رحمتك مصيرنا ومآلنا واصبب سجال عفوك على ذنوبنا ومن علينا بإصلاح عيوبنا واجعل التقوى زادنا وفي دينك اجتهادنا وعليك توكلنا واعتمادنا. أللهم ثبتنا على نهج الاستقامة وأعذنا في الدنيا من موجبات الندامة يوم القيامة وخفف عنا ثقل الأوزار وارزقنا عيشة الأبرار واكفنا واصرف عنا شر الأشرار وأعتق رقابنا ورقاب آبائنا وأمهاتنا وإخواننا وأخواتنا من النار برحمتك يا عزيز يا غفار يا كريم يا ستار يا عليم يا جبار يا الله يا الله برحمتك يا أرحم الراحمين و يا أول الأولين ويا آخر الآخرين ويا ذا القوة المتين ويا راحم المساكين ويا أرحم الراحمين لا إله إلا أنتسبحانك إني كنت من الظالمين. وصلى اللهعلى سيدنا محمد وآله وصحبه أجمعين والحمد لله رب العالمين".